||| | ||||||| || |||| ||| ||| |||
I0165025

Exorcism In A Brand New Way

By Brett Connell

Copyright © 2016 Brett Connell

All rights reserved. No part of this publication may be reproduced, distributed, or transmitted in any form or by any means, including photocopying, recording, or other electronic or mechanical methods, without the prior written permission of the publisher, except in the case of brief quotations embodied in critical reviews and certain other noncommercial uses permitted by copyright law.

Amplified Bible (AMP)
Copyright © 2015 by The Lockman Foundation, La Habra, CA 90631. All rights reserved.

Scripture quotations marked NIV are taken from the Holy Bible, NEW INTERNATIONAL VERSION®, NIV® Copyright © 1973, 1978, 1984, 2011 by Biblica, Inc.® Used by permission. All rights reserved worldwide.

NEW INTERNATIONAL VERSION® and NIV® are registered trademarks of Biblica, Inc. Use of either trademark for the offering of goods or services requires the prior written consent of Biblica US, Inc.

Scripture taken from the New King James Version®. Copyright © 1982 by Thomas Nelson. Used by permission. All rights reserved.

ISBN 9780997454123

Contact the Author
Brett Connell
shiningyourglory@gmx.com

Previous works from Brett Connell:
A Remembrance [2015]   ISBN: 9780997454116
Heavens Courts [2016]   ISBN: 9780997454109

Special thanks to: Jesus Christ, Nancy Connell, Evangelist Barbara Lynch, Reverend Christopher Gore, Duncan & Lynda Connell. Thank you so much for all the support, encouragement and help in making this book possible.

Brett is a servant of Christ in The Lighthouse Inc. Church of Wyoming, Delaware – Pastored by Evangelist Barbara Lynch.

Table of Contents

Preface

In the deliverance ministry, we have seen many new and incredible things that God has shown us that we have not seen or heard of before. There is a depth to the realm of deliverance and exorcism that is being unearthed at this given time to reveal to the saints the deep works of freedom in Christ.

This knowledge is giving us many invaluable tools and resources to utilize in Christ as we go forth to set the captives free in Jesus' name.

Some of the things that God has shown us have been so amazing it is hard to believe, but as God reveals the knowledge and mechanics behind the scenes it begins to make sense as the Holy Spirit sheds light onto these deeper truths and we are in awe of the magnitude of God's wisdom.

In this book, I will give testimonials of actual deliverance and exorcism sessions that I have participated in and a breakdown of everything that God has shown us. All of the names that I use in this book have been changed to protect the identities of those to whom we ministered.

The purpose of this book is to teach and share with everyone the amazing things God is doing to set people free in these current times. I want to share this to as many people as possible and we pray that they will connect with God in this deeper level and use these strategies in setting other captives free.

God will use the members of a deliverance team in a unique way according to each person's gifts and anointing. We are all members of the same body and though we serve different functions and capacities, we all must work together in unity. This is the foundation of any work for God – unity. It is essential to operate by the influence of the Holy Spirit.

Our team consists of seer prophets and all are anointed by God for deliverance ministry. God shows the team visions and speaks to us directly while addressing various aspects of deliverance and exorcism. He will use the gifts and personalities that He gave us to do His work in setting the captives free.

There are some in the Body who know about the ins and outs of exorcism but there are many who do not. This book is written in such a way that it will break down and explain everything God has shown us through the different stories of each deliverance and exorcism session we have participated in the last few years. I believe this will help every level of person whether they have a little or a great amount of expertise in this field.

I also want to be upfront about deliverance and exorcisms. In years past, the word used to describe what has been happening in setting people free has changed. The term used to describe setting captives free was 'deliverance'. There was a measure of healing, restoration and the anointing of God would drive unclean spirits out of people. In summation, Jesus showed up and God's presence set captives free. They were ministered to, given new mindsets to live out their new freedom and walked with God.

In these end times however we are seeing latter-day, end-time demons being released from hell that are immensely more powerful than they ever were before. While deliverance is still fully active today – what we are doing now is all-out exorcisms. It is the same thing as before but on a much larger scale. Demons are fully manifesting in people and they are strong. Nevertheless, Jesus is always faithful – the angels of God are at the ready (if you call upon them) to assist in binding and restraining those spirits and sending them to the pit.

I am also well aware that many people will cry foul at the hearing of the fact that we participate in deliverance and exorcism. I respect each denomination of the gospel of Christ and I will not speak against any of them, and I will not engage in any argument with anyone who disagrees with what we do. I can tell you that Jesus Christ told me in the bible that I read that I can do what I do:

[Mark 16:17-18] **17** These signs will accompany those who have believed: in My name they will cast out demons, they will speak in new tongues; **18** they will pick up serpents, and if they drink anything deadly, it will not hurt them; they will lay hands on the sick, and they will get well." (AMP)

I have authority and am certified to do these works by Jesus Christ and the freedom that He brings as He uses *any* vessel to do these works; and that is the testimony of its effectiveness and validity.

Having said that, I also want to establish that the revelations that God has given us and the new way in which God is moving to set captives free is seemingly 'radical' and quite unique. Yet this is the way that God is moving in this hour and we will not put Him in a box!

I would also like to note for the people who do not know much about exorcism: it is not as Hollywood has portrayed it. Some movies have been made to depict or otherwise represent exorcisms in the most contrary, skewed and negative light. Unfortunately, this is the first thing many people think of when they hear the word exorcism.

A true exorcism is the power and anointing of God driving an unclean spirit up to the surface of a person and commanding it to leave in Jesus' name. It is no different from what Jesus did in the bible, and it is possible for you and me to do this because the bible says we can. However, I strongly suggest that you yourself get cleaned up first and rid your life of any sin nature and walk closely with God and strive to live the holy life before you begin any kind of exorcism.

I say this because when I was in training I still had many demons inside of me – and during one deliverance session the demons in the man we were working on came after the demons inside of me in a territorial battle and they threw me up against the wall and dragged me around the room. It was quite an experience. There was also another time a demon manifested in a man and almost broke my thumb. I strongly urge everyone to rid yourselves of demons before you actively engage in this procedure and know who you are in Christ. Please, do not end up like the seven sons of Sceva:

[Acts 19:13-16] **13** Then some of the traveling Jewish exorcists also attempted to call the name of the Lord Jesus over those who had evil spirits, saying, "I implore you and solemnly command you by the Jesus whom Paul preaches!" **14** Seven sons of one [named] Sceva, a Jewish chief priest, were doing this. **15** But the evil spirit retorted, "I know and recognize and acknowledge Jesus, and I know about Paul, but as for you, who are you?" **16** Then the man, in whom was the evil spirit, leaped on them and subdued all of them and overpowered them, so that they ran out of that house [in terror, stripped] naked and wounded. (AMP)

It requires a close, personal and deep walk with Christ for Him to abide in us in the measure we need for participating in exorcisms. We may all say that we have Christ in us, but does Jesus have us in Him? We need to evaluate where we are really at and be honest with ourselves. Is there enough of God in us that demons have to yield to our commands? Or do the demons see the sin in our lives and laugh at our faith?

Having said all this, it is my prayer and my hope that you will glean much from this book and that this revelation knowledge can help you in some way. As the darkness in this world gets worse by the day, God will increase His light and make it available to those who are willing to receive it and utilize it.

Whether you are seeking to set yourself free, or further your own ministry with this revelation from God, I pray that the Holy Spirit would minister to you as you read forward and reveal even greater and deeper revelations to you that you may take to the world in Jesus' name.

Chapter 1: The Breakdown of Satan's Tactics

It was the first time I met Tim at all when he showed up for his deliverance session today. He came in and we sat down to talk and ease the atmosphere with light conversation about what God is doing in his life and where he's at spiritually.

Any time someone comes into The Lighthouse there is an anointing already here and the presence of God is strong. Under this anointing much pain began to manifest inside of Tim. He started talking about his previous experiences in churches where he was wronged and felt slighted.

He told me that it wasn't right that many pastors and churches would exploit the gifting's of other people for personal gain or that if they saw someone being used by God in a "better" way than themselves they would treat them poorly or put them down so they don't grow past their own prideful levels of recognition and praise.

He told me that he believed it is really about the souls of people and not who is greater or more important or has better gifts. I concurred with him and talked about what had happened to him that caused him to feel this way.

Through our dialogue, it appeared that the churches he went to were corrupted in leadership to some degree, or at least not operating in unity. The jealousy among staff was obvious and one was always trying to outdo the other. He spoke of watching people desperately seek God by entering the house of the Lord and begin to feel secure until the wolves in sheep's clothing struck; and set them back to the point they left the church worse off than when they first entered.

He could not understand why people would do such things if they truly professed to know God and follow Him. They all look and act as if they are in the Spirit but their hearts show otherwise.

Without recognizing it himself, his face shifted slightly and the tone of his voice changed. He began to question why these things happen and how could they be allowed to happen in the first place. The look in his eyes was different – this was now another personality that had manifested that I was now speaking with. It was still Tim, but a different Tim, with a different set of characteristics and beliefs. This

Tim was less concerned about the souls and more concerned with questioning God.

This is known as an "alter" which is short for "alternate personality". This is literally a normal, functional part of the human brain that was split due to trauma or severe pain.

Alters form when there is a serious trauma or pain that occurs in someone's life and they are unable or unwilling to process that pain or understand what is happening at that given time. Because it is so overwhelming, the mind will split and portions of that pain and trauma get pushed off to the side to be dealt with in various ways such as burying it, rationalizing it, isolating it or compartmentalizing it.

This occurs so that the brain can process what has happened in a smaller portion that it can handle so as not to cause a sort of sensory input overload or cause a complete mental breakdown.

I knew at this time I was speaking with a fragmented piece of Tim's mind – an alter – and it was hurt deeply. After he spoke, I prayed with him and released the holy angels to go into Tim's mind and minister to this broken fragment of his mind. I sent the angels there to minister truth into his consciousness regarding his situations.

When speaking to an alter, we pray with them and speak to them as though they were the real person – because essentially they are. I prayed aloud with Tim and I spoke to the alter, addressing the issues without directly confronting Tim. I was led to do this because in his mind I was another churchgoer that could very likely cause him pain. I did not want the alter to engage defense mechanisms and shut down our conversation because of any perceived threat to Tim.

I prayed that the angels would minister to that alter and show him the truth about the situations of his circumstances. I explained that bad things happen to good people because of sin. People had sinned and that allowed demons to enter them and heavily influence their thoughts and actions. Because those people did not repent or strive to follow God's word, the doors were left open and the demons were passed down to future generations – gaining strength as each generation progressed. Curses were activated and wrought destruction on people's lives as a consequence for disobedience and not following God's word.

Because of this, demons had legal rights to oppress and afflict people and even children. That it was someone's duty to stand in the gap, repent for these iniquities, and strive to follow God's word and use the Kingdom authority to break these curses and expel these demons and speak the blessings of God into people's lives and walk closely with God to cover their loved ones in hedges of protection.

I told Tim that because no one did this in his family line, he himself was tormented in this way and that is the answer to his questions. His hope came in the form of knowing that he himself could serve God and use Kingdom authority to break these curses and expel the demons from his own life and then his lineage to stop this demonic repetitive cycle. That God never left him nor forsook him, but rather was leading him all the way through his life – down in the mud with him, even carrying him on His back at times through the trenches of demonic warfare – all to bring him to this place for understanding and revelation from Heaven to answer all his questions. That the answer itself was inside of him, through Jesus.

At this, you could see relief on Tim's face. In his eyes, you could see a washing taking place on the inside as all the lies of the enemy were prayed out of his mind – praying that angels would remove every dagger from his mind that seeped poisonous lies into his thought life and eventually worked their way into his belief system.

The alter begins to feel comfortable knowing it can have peace and so can the rest of Tim – and it no longer needs to protect him or any of his other parts, because it now knows and trusts in Jesus and Tim's core's ability (the real Tim God made) to follow Jesus and learn to engage in spiritual warfare.

Once the alter is convinced that its function and purposes were validated and finished, it can release those broken mind fragments to Christ for healing and restoration. The alter is guided to Jesus where it is healed and restored and then reintegrated back into Tim's personality for wholeness and soundness of mind.

God heals the pain and removes the triggers and demonic systems behind the trauma so that the only thing left is a clean memory of the events that can be used to minister to others without negative emotions surfacing – for the purpose of bringing souls into the Kingdom.

The plan and design is that through Christ, everything that we deal with and go through can be used as a tool to minister to others who are suffering in that pain and are not yet healed. The truth is, we are never really healed until we understand the purpose behind the pain.

Once Tim was fully healed in this area, it was on to the next thing that God was showing us in this session. Tim had a heart full of wounds from the Body of Christ in particular, with all the backbiting, fighting, strife, discord and contention he encountered in his experiences.

This is one of the greatest strategies of the enemy.

When God was trying to get my attention back in 2011, I experienced a very powerful vision from God. It was the first time I had been taken out of body through a divine encounter. I was taken into a church building somewhere in California, and I sat among the people in the congregation. I heard the people gossiping and slandering the others in the room, quietly talking and whispering amongst themselves.

I watched bitterness and jealousy travel around the sanctuary with shifty eyes and shady glances and looks of contempt on the people's faces, but no confrontation ever ensued. When people locked eyes, their faces were plastered with rehearsed smiles and jovial greetings, all the while daggers were coming out of their eyes.

The couple in front of me were both sitting in wheelchairs, and the one man suddenly got up from the chair and everyone gasped as though a miracle had taken place – but he turned to his partner, also wheelchair bound, and told her that he lied about being disabled and only did this to deceive and take advantage of her in some way.

I could not believe I was in the house of God – but at this point, something even worse happened. A man who was very finely dressed, middle-aged but still very handsome and proper stood at the pulpit in the altar wearing a clean and prim business suit. He stood there with his arms folded across his chest with an arrogant smug smile on his face as though he owned this place – and pure evil came out of his eyes that was so heavy I fell to my knees and eventually onto the floor under the weight of evil and power. The air became so thick I could not breathe. I glanced up again toward him, he lorded over this place, and I knew he was the devil himself sitting comfortably in the house of God, right behind the pulpit.

I understood what Tim was saying about the people in the house of God. But ultimately this initial misleading was not the people's fault – because those pastors and leaders are not living the word of God and are deceiving many with their false teachings and doctrines. There are many leaders and pastors not preaching the full truth and are allowing the multitudes to be led astray by the enemy. However, there is a personal responsibility that rests upon the individuals themselves to check what they hear against the word of God. Every person likely has access to their own bible, and most people can read.

By the grace of God, Tim was not led astray in this context, but he was affected all the same by being beaten down by this demonic system to the point that he resigned himself to sit down and be a nobody who just heard the word and did no works for God.

Perhaps the enemy could not take him out; by the grace of God, but the next best strategy was to cause him to be hurt so bad that he gave up and sat down. A child of God who sits in a seat and just listens is no threat to the enemy or his kingdom of darkness. The devil will gladly allow them to come to church and hear the word, and he will even sit right next to them and not bat an eye.

Another alter surfaced on Tim's face and in his eyes… he was truly comfortable and determined that his path and goal was to sit down and just exist in the house of God.

In dealing with this alter inside of Tim, we utilized information that we knew of the real (core) Tim. (We will refer to the true and whole person of Tim as the core). Core Tim loves God with all his heart and wants to do the greater works Jesus talks about in the bible.

I ministered to this wounded alter by reminding him of the word of God and how we should participate in a season of learning and growing, but that also we should be applying and living what we know in the word. I prayed and asked God to heal those wounds in the heart and to minister truth upon those hardened layers of scar tissue over his spiritual heart. As the alter softened up, we reminded him and the core that God's will for us is to love and serve Him with all our mind. That meant each part of the mind had to come together for this purpose – and this was sufficient to trigger the alter into letting go of its defense mechanisms and allowing God's healing power to touch core Tim and restore this fragmented piece of the mind to wholeness.

In many cases, the alters have been created to protect the core from additional pain or damage. There are so many types of alters that can serve literally any function or purpose inside a person's mind. We will see more about this as this book progresses.

As core Tim surfaced and began to express his thankfulness to God, you could tell there was a genuine driving force behind his love for God and his willingness to serve Him. The Holy Spirit opened our eyes to see this; but also that there was something off about the way he was crying out to God. Holy Spirit showed us that there was a fear inside that was also driving him.

The bible tells us that fear is not of God because fear has to do with punishment. It also tells us that if we love God, we will obey all His commands. We do this out of love, and we serve and love Him because He first loved us.

But there was a part of Tim's soul that was serving God out of a fear. God told us that his soul was being held captive in a region of captivity in hell.

Yes, we can have parts or fragments of our soul bound in hell while we are still alive and born again filled with the Holy Spirit. That is because our soul is our mind, will and emotions. This part of our being is not immune to demonic attack or possession. These are our thoughts, our choices and our feelings. If you mean to say the devil cannot get into your thoughts, choices or feelings then you must be walking on water.

When a believer is born again and filled with the Holy Spirit – it is their spirit-man that is filled and sanctified and reconnected with God through the blood of Christ by faith. Demons cannot enter your spirit-man at this point but they can still oppress it and cause trouble all around about it. Our spirit-man can also be bruised, wounded and broken.

We did not get into sin overnight – and you are not going to be set free from countless and very powerful generational demonic strongholds and legal rights overnight either. See where I am going with this? I am not saying God cannot do that – I am addressing the truth that Christians can have demons and there is a difference between soul and spirit that many people misunderstand.

Let us go back and see what God did with Tim. So God told us that part of his soul was held in bondage in a region of captivity in hell. This had to do with a fear inside of him that was partly a foundation to his willingness to serve God.

God showed us that 12 generations ago on his mothers' side of the family, there was a person who committed horrible acts of sin. Even though they repented and received forgiveness, there was something in them that caused them to never forgive themselves for what had happened. Because of this choice and belief, a stronghold in the mind was formed that they had to beat themselves up and walk under condemnation in order to be accepted by God. They believed God wanted them punished and to suffer for their mistakes before He would forgive them, and that God would never forget that sin and always hold it over their head as a tool to use against them.

This belief system and stronghold of the mind created a house for a demon of condemnation to enter in and pass down through the generational line into all the descendants. Because this was never caught and dealt with, it continued to this day, getting stronger and stronger.

By this generation, a spirit of fear had joined in with the spirit of condemnation and caused the person to suffer a fear of judgment, fear of hell, fear of punishment and fear of death.

These were now factors in Tim's drive to serve God – out of fear rather than out of love.

It didn't stop here, though. God showed us in the Spirit that his soul was locked in a prison cell of condemnation also.

While it was true that demons of fear were driving Tim to think and feel this way, the root of the problem was the part of his soul locked in captivity. In other words, the demons of fear could be cast out of him but if the root of the problem was left undealt with, then the base of condemnation could serve as an open door to allow different types of spirits to enter in and influence Tim.

Perhaps if someone keeps returning for deliverance as though it seems they are doing something to allow spirits to constantly return – it is advisable to seek God to determine if the root of the problem is truly being addressed and dealt with or not.

We prayed together and called upon the angels of God to assist us as we descended into the regions of hell where his soul was being held captive. We took the key of David and opened up the prison cell holding his soul captive and pulled him out and cut off any cords from hell and any ungodly influences through soul ties.

We released the fire of God into the strongholds of the mind as we ministered truth from the Scriptures. After pulling this part of his soul out of the generational prison cell of condemnation, we destroyed the prison.

We also stood in the gap for the person who committed the original sin 12 generations ago on his mothers' side. We held them up before the Lord and repented on their behalf for any sin or iniquity that was participated in or continued. We asked God to release His forgiveness upon their sins and wash the iniquity with the blood of Jesus – and then close the doorway to the curses that originated from that sin.

Now that they have been repented for and forgiveness has been released, the blood of Jesus cleanses the sin and washes away all unrighteousness. The demons no longer have a legal right to operate through that doorway or through the curses. We then broke the curses off his life from this root of iniquity by the power of the Holy Spirit and the blood of Jesus. We sent fire down the generational line to purge it through this root network and system. After this, we had to address and confront the demons that were operating behind these curses, pains and traumas.

There is some background history that we need to touch briefly to explain what is happening in the realm of deliverance. Many years ago, ministers were performing what we call deliverances to cast out demons and heal the sick. The core of deliverance has not changed but there are several factors that have impacted the realm of deliverance over the years.

In years past, many ministers found that demons would flee at the name of Jesus under the anointing of God. While this is pretty much the summation of what happens in deliverance, there have been several factors that affect this that we will go into.

Firstly, we are looking at the condition of the world that we are in. We know that sin empowers demons, and this world is getting increasingly dark by the day. Just look at newspaper headlines and watch the news on TV to catch a glimpse of how bad the state of mankind has become. Now imagine to yourself, would you have seen these kinds of headlines and newscasts back in 1950? Darkness has increased exponentially in only the last 70 years. Compare that to all the times beforehand, and you'll notice a stark contrast between the rate of growth in darkness from then until the last 70 years.

In fact the bible speaks of this time and season we are in right now:

[Isaiah 60:2] See, darkness covers the earth and thick darkness is over the peoples, but the Lord rises upon you and his glory appears over you. (NIV)

If you could only see into the spirit realm and behold the massive powers of darkness and all their devices, strongholds and principalities looming over this earth and every structure of authority and government, highly organized and unified to influence man to further any agenda of the kingdom of darkness – you would truly shudder at the level of warfare we are all engaged in but few realize.

We are no longer doing mere deliverances. We are doing full-blown exorcisms on the people and we are tapping into such a grand depth of the spirit realm and seeing so many facets of the spirit realm that it is mind-boggling. However, God wants us to see these things, to know them and understand them so that we are properly equipped to fight the gross darkness that has unfolded across the earth and continues to get worse in the days ahead.

The reason we have migrated into exorcisms is because of the increase of sin and darkness, the demons have gotten much stronger. Whereas before they would come out screaming at the name of Jesus, now they are more fortified and reluctant to leave and they have great power to make attempts to resist. Not only this, but they are operating on a legal system and in some cases they do not have to leave. There are many systems of demonic empires inside people that work with each other – and demons will throw up lesser ones to confuse ministers and pretend to be gone all the while hiding behind pain and trauma and other kingdoms of demons.

It truly takes the Spirit of the living God to show and explain the entire process to ensure that everything is dealt with accordingly. That every root is taken out and every source removed so that a complete and pure works is done in the people.

Now, going back to Tim, I had just finished ministering to two alters and God was flushing out pain and healing the inner parts of his mind and heart. All the groundwork was dealt with and anything the demons could try to hide behind was removed. At this juncture God led me to deal with the spirits.

Demons of condemnation, fear, judgment and fear of death were lingering inside of him.

These spirits had nowhere to hide, nothing to protect them as far as strongholds, as God already dealt with several factors:

1. Alters (alternate personalities) can sometimes adopt feelings and belief systems that aid demons and give them places to hide in or operate from, including legal rights to stay inside the person. They must be ministered to and convinced to let go of their function and persuaded that the core of the person will be protected and healed.

2. Lies that we believe to be truth (strongholds in the mind) where demons can stay undetected as they attach to your beliefs and operate behind pain that you may have stored up in your soul. Such strongholds are only broken by the truth of the word of God that is ministered correctly to address the foundation of the lie and replace it with the truth.

3. Open wounds in the heart that are still there from unresolved issues or ongoing circumstances of pain and trauma. These are healed by God, filled with the Holy Spirit and ministered to the people giving them truth, hope and faith to overcome and forgive and release anything to God

that the enemy could use to establish strongholds.

4. Spiritual devices and weapons that exist in the spirit realm and operate against a person's body/soul/spirit. These are real weapons and devices, chambers, prisons, instruments, landscapes, etc. that have purposes and functions designed to bind, hinder or otherwise steal, kill and destroy.

At this rate the demons were commanded to leave in Jesus' name and they left more easily than they would had these others not been dealt with first. Jesus won the victory and Tim was set free from this first round of bondage.

After each round of expulsion of demons to the pit, we anoint the person with oil, seal the works God did in the blood of Jesus, and fill them with the Holy Spirit. The idea is that after being emptied of this demonic junk, they should be filled with Holy Spirit in those places.

The core Tim was surfaced once again and expressed how wonderful he felt after Jesus did all this work on him. He told us that he felt so much lighter, total peace and a renewed spirit.

Chapter 2: Behind The Scenes In The Spirit Realm

We worked on a man we will call Joshua. Joshua was a doctor and had a lot of medical expertise, but also understood that some problems are strictly spiritual. As we proceeded to work with him, we saw that there were demons attempting to cut his life short through curses of death.

The Holy Spirit led us to break the curses of death over his life that came in through ancestral idol worship, generational murder and sacrifice of children and sorcery. We repented on behalf of those that participated in these horrible abominations and released Joshua from the curse and consequence of those sins.

We also had to break curses off Joshua pertaining to words that he spoke over himself. What he experienced was a seeming failure of anything he tried to do. Even striving to serve God, it felt like nothing he ever did worked right or just ended up in failure.

The words he spoke over himself were phrases such as, 'I can't ever get it right' and 'you did it again Josh, just like every time'.

These words have power in them – and the enemy is right there to enforce what he can with those negative words over his life. These words caused a curse of failure and defeat to apply to his life and therefore demons can enter and operate in that curse to cause the havoc and destruction in his life to bring the curse to its fullest effect.

We had Joshua repent for the negative words that he spoke over himself and ask God to forgive him. Once the curse was broken, we commanded the spirits behind the curse to depart as well.

There was also a scrambler spirit attached to Joshua's mind. A scrambler spirit is something that takes what other people say and do – and twists it to make the person perceive those words/actions in a skewed and offensive manner.

A scrambler spirit can also twist what God is saying to the person and cause confusion or deception. It can cause a severe misunderstanding of the word of God and lead people astray. It can function to destroy a person's walk with God, families, relationships and businesses.

We see evidence in the bible that God Himself can dispatch a lying spirit into the mouths of prophets to speak lies with the intent of causing that person to follow the spoken words to their death – of course this being a judgment against king Ahab for his rebellion and sin.

[1 Kings 22:19-23] **19** Micaiah said, "Therefore, hear the word of the Lord. I saw the Lord sitting on His throne, and all the host (army) of heaven standing by Him on His right hand and on His left. **20** The Lord said, 'Who will entice Ahab to go up and fall at Ramoth-gilead?' And one said this, while another said that. **21** Then a spirit came forward and stood before the Lord and said, 'I will entice him.' **22** The Lord said to him, 'How?' And he said, 'I will go out and be a deceiving spirit in the mouth of all his prophets.' Then the Lord said, 'You are to entice him and also succeed. Go and do so.' **23** Now then, behold, the Lord has put a deceiving spirit in the mouth of all these prophets; and the Lord has proclaimed disaster against you." (AMP)

If God can do this in His sovereignty and His purpose in judgment, how much more will an evil spirit desire to do such a thing to a person?

These spiritual forces can serve any innumerable functions and purposes. This shows us that these demonic influences have the potential to affect every area of our lives. This is why it is written in the word of God:

[Ephesians 6:12] For our struggle is not against flesh and blood [contending only with physical opponents], but against the rulers, against the powers, against the world forces of this [present] darkness, against the spiritual forces of wickedness in the heavenly (supernatural) places. (AMP)

How is it that spirits get assigned to curses and know what functions to serve and assignments to carry out against the person? The kingdom of darkness is highly organized and has a ranking system. There are also 'thrones and dominions' (i.e. positions of authority and seats of power) that exist within the enemy's kingdom.

God has shown us four types of demons to bind before every exorcism and deliverance session:

1. The Organizer of Witchcraft
2. The Strongman over Generations
3. The Generational Gatekeeper
4. The Purveyor of Curses

These are four positions of operation that the kingdom of darkness uses over people's lives. Each position is filled by a spirit that operates in the capacity of its title.

The Organizer of Witchcraft is a spirit that gathers together any and all witchcraft that is available in the atmosphere over that person. It searches out any witchcraft prayers or other destructive methods that would attempt or seek to come against that person.

Once it gathers these, it then utilizes them and distributes those tasks to other lesser demons under its authority.

The Strongman over Generations does a similar thing although it's realm of jurisdiction is entirely within that person's bloodline, generation and ancestry. This spirit collects and utilizes any and all legal rights that exist in the bloodline for spirits to enter and operate against the person. This strongman works with the Gatekeeper who can assign demons and give assignments based on the evil within the bloodline of the person that it receives from the Strongman.

The purveyor of curses deals specifically with any and all curses found in the atmosphere, bloodline and generations.

If these spirits are allowed to operate in the exorcism session it will make things increasingly difficult. One of the main keys is to send angels to fight and resist the powers and principalities in the heavenlies over the region and territory. We also must send out angels to bind any and all strongmen and ruler spirits that would operate in that region where the session is taking place.

[Mark 3:27] But no one can go into a strong man's house and steal his property unless he first overpowers *and* ties up the strong man, and then he will ransack *and* rob his house. (AMP)

Having taken these necessary steps, the spirits manifest more quickly and receive less aid and assistance as well as power and strength from other spirits in the person or vicinity.

We then commanded the scrambler spirit to manifest itself – and we cut the cords of control it had attached to Joshua's mind and separated this spirit from his soul with the sword of the Spirit.

[Ephesians 6:17] And take … the sword of the Spirit, which is the Word of God. (AMP)

[Hebrews 4:12] For the word of God … is sharper than any two-edged sword, penetrating as far as the division of the soul and spirit [the completeness of a person] … (AMP)

God showed us that in addition to this spirit possessing Joshua, there were tools and devices that this spirit was using against him in the spirit realm. What we saw was a giant rake screeching down a blackboard. This loud and crippling noise was resonating throughout his ear gates (spiritually) and flooding his hearing with noise and therefore reducing his ability to hear God (or any sound reasoning for that matter). See figure 1a.

God also showed us in the spirit realm how there were demons that had Joshua convinced that the things he was doing was called of God – and that all these works were accomplishing great feats for His kingdom. Sadly, Joshua had a religious mindset that by works he could earn his salvation and right standing with God. These demons had him deceived and even manipulated and controlled what he did in all kinds of ways, and spiritually had him on a puppet string to influence his moves – all the while laughing at Joshua and his lack of awareness to what was happening to him in the spirit realm. See figure 1b.

[Isaiah 64:6] For we all have become like one who is [ceremonially] unclean [like a leper], And all our deeds of righteousness are like filthy rags; We all wither and decay like a leaf, And our wickedness [our sin, our injustice, our wrongdoing], like the wind, takes us away [carrying us far from God's favor, toward destruction]. (AMP)

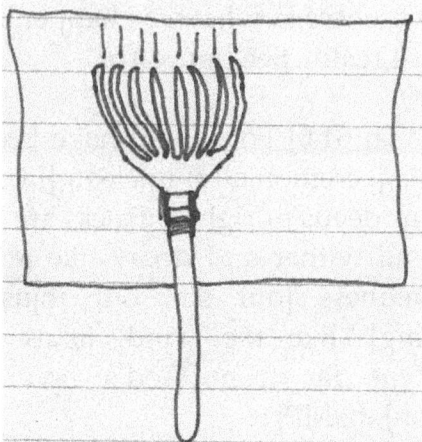

Rake screeching down
chalk board.
(scrambler Spirit)
Flooding the ear gates
with Noise.

Fig. 1a

Demons are laughing hysterically at ▓▓▓▓ and all the religious groups around him — totally manipulating these people to do "works" for God but it's not God.

Demons

Fig. 1b

We had begun to call upon the angels of God to remove this rake device and cut the strings off this puppet system as we commanded the demons to be bound in Jesus' name. The demons reacted within Joshua and began to manifest in his face and we assigned the angels to torment these demon spirits (and restrain them) until they went into the abyss and completely dislodged themselves from Joshua's soul.

Upon the departure of these evil spirits from Joshua, angels came forward and ministered restoration to his soul where these wounding's took place. God placed a lace band of light around his head and we saw in the spirit that light going into his mind and cleansing what damage had been done.

Joshua now experienced freedom from demonic spirits but also needed ministering to clear up beliefs and mindsets that he had that were based in deception or falsehood. Demons can leave a person but if their beliefs and habits never change, the door is always open for them to come back in. It takes the truth (word of God) to tear down those strongholds of the mind and break the lies of the enemy. Only the renewed mind in Christ can be the solid foundation for the mind to stay afloat in the Spirit of God.

An important part of a person's wellbeing is realigning their three-part being together in the correct order. In case you were wondering, that is the body, soul and spirit of a person.

There is an order to which these things are to be placed in to function properly and effectively. The correct order is that a person's body is to be disciplined to sit down and line up under the soul. The soul is then disciplined to sit down and line up under the spirit-man; which is then directly under the Holy Spirit.

In this way, the Holy Spirit has direct and full access to our spirit-man which is where God dwells in us and where we have the ability to walk in the Spirit of God and experience Him in His fullness.

If the soul (mind, will and emotions) or the body (physical desires and fallen nature) stands in the way of our spirit-man and the Holy Spirit, we are cutting ourselves off of God in varying degrees and measures depending upon how out of sync our parts are.

We saw this model after something God had shown us in a vision. (see Fig. 1c)

I saw a vision of telephone poles extremely high up in the air with the wires broken at one end dangling down with sparking electricity as though the current was cut off or limited. With this person in particular, we were having a blockage dealing with healing of soul fragments. It was apparent we could not minister healing to the soul and God showed us why.

The telephone poles represented this persons soul. They were built extremely high into the air, therefore it was impossible for someone to service them. Their thoughts, desires, fleshly and carnal lusts were exalted above normal and this created the problem we currently faced.

The wires were weathered and broken, the body was in a condition of sickness because of the damages and wounds occurring within the soul. The body could not prosper in health if the soul was living a lifestyle that invited curses for rebellion and disobedience to God's word.

Lastly, the electricity current moving through the wires represented the spirit-man of the person. The amount of amperage or force behind the electricity represented the Holy Spirit's ability to move freely in this system. Obviously, it was lacking severely.

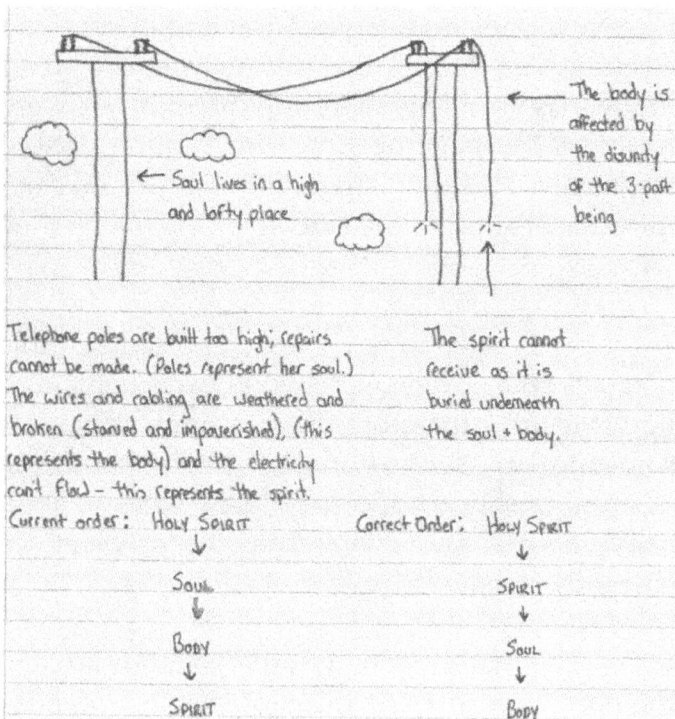

Fig. 1c

This person was in desperate need of a realignment of their three part being. It would be quite difficult to continue to operate in this fashion – and it made us all wonder if a similar problem existed within each one of us?

We discovered a prayer that would help us with this realignment, coupled with the continued deliverance.

We prayed for the Lord Jesus to assist us in the realignment of our three part being: we commanded our bodies to sit down and line up under our souls. We then commanded our souls to sit down and line up under our spirit-man. Then we asked Jesus to help us in realigning out spirit-man under the Holy Spirit.

It is a co-labor with Jesus, meaning that we have our own part to play in this. We stay in the Spirit by striving to live holy and removing sin from our lives through living the word and keeping a full and consistent prayer and fasting lifestyle. We must have love as our foundation and be fully obedient to God in all areas of our life.

As we live in this way, we can retain the alignment we seek to have in the correct order. What is the importance of this order?

If you look at it this way – when in prayer and you are trying to focus on God but then suddenly the thought of the roast in the oven takes you out of the Spirit and causes you to run into the kitchen to check and see if in fact you had one in the oven or not – is an example of your soul being higher than your spirit-man.

If you're in intercessory prayer and your focused on what God is leading you to pray, then your hangnail accidentally gets caught on your shirt nubs and pulls a tear in your skin and it causes you to nurse your wound and fall out of prayer – your body is likely aligned well above your spirit-man.

Any time God deposits something into you, it goes into your spirit-man. This is where you pick up on things from God. Your spirit-man is what communicates with God in the spirit realm. This is like the primary facility in our walk with God. If something is blocking, binding or hindering this, it spells big trouble for our communication with God.

Our spirit-man is the very first thing cleansed and purified by God when we are born again and it is the Holy Spirit that takes up residence inside us – whereby perfecting our spirit man to accommodate His presence within us.

As you can see from these deliverances, the body and soul remain possessed and wounded even after having become born again.

This is the importance of our deliverance and freedom – it is something we have to work at daily. This is a lifestyle we must strive to live that goes against the grain of the world. Jesus wasn't kidding when He told us to pick up our cross and follow him daily. He wasn't kidding when He said we would be persecuted for His namesake.

That persecution isn't limited to some divine end-time insanity where people are chasing Christians with pitchforks and torches.

There is plenty of persecution available today if you would actually truly live the word of God in its fullness each and every day.

Chapter 3: Devices, Fragmentation And Captivity

We were working on a lady named Tori who came to us because she was under severe witchcraft attack.

A spirit of infirmity was sent to attack her mind and cause much mental distress. These attacks were so thick and heavy against her that she began to consider the possibility that she was mentally insane.

God showed us in the spirit realm many of the sinister and evil devices which were attached to her physical brain and then explained to us the function and operation of these devices.

We saw a sort of metal strainer (colander) around her head. This device was reflecting any kind of healing or ministering of the Word to penetrate any of her gates. This was also symbolic of the 'head' being cut off and starved of receiving any spiritual nutrients whereby the 'body' would wither away and eventually die spiritually.

There were ties into her mind from aliens (which are demons) and allowed an open door to astral projection inside her mind. These doorways were closed as we called Tori up to repent for any involvement in alien research, UFO obsession and any potential contact with UFO sightings, etc.

We also saw deeper into this metal dome device that encapsulated her head. Underneath of that was another device, a system of sorts.

We saw a large nuclear reactor. There were large carbon control rods that sunk deep into the inner workings of her mind. These rods were stopping any and all reactions taking place from the Holy Spirit. It was as though the Spirit of God was the source of power, generating energy and reactions within her spirit-man but yet these control rods sunk deep into her inner being to absorb and slow down those reactions and energies to a crawl and eventually a standstill.

God showed us this; and told us to remove those carbon control rods slowly from the mind and from around her spirit-man, whereby allowing that Holy Spirit reaction to take effect within her vessel and generate a solid flow of power into her once again.

To see what we saw in the spirit in regards to the metal strainer device around her head, see Fig. 2a.

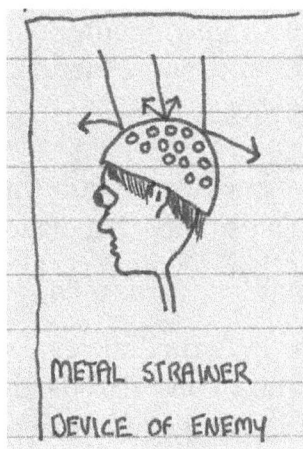

METAL STRAINER
DEVICE OF ENEMY

Fig. 2a

I did not draw any diagram or illustration of the reactor device and control rods, God did not lead me to draw that and I won't necessarily draw it after-the-fact because the anointing to do that was present in that exorcism session and is not present outside of that context.

We have to remember that the anointing must be present to do these things if it's really from God. We can't do anything without the anointing of God. Otherwise it's just words and scribbles with no value.

God instructed us to release His light into the mind after those devices were removed, and to cover all 4 lobes of the brain (frontal, parietal, occipital and temporal) in the Blood of Jesus. Having done this, spirits manifested of mental torment, mental illness, schizophrenia and dementia.

Those spirits were cast out by Jesus and sent to the pit. Afterwards, God did a major surgery on her mind and ministered much healing into these parts of her brain.

Tori can now function much better than she could in the past, as the spiritual side of these things were dealt with. The only thing left for Tori to do was to retain her freedom and deliverance daily, and work on changing her mindsets and thought patterns with her new horizons and borders.

One thing we see so often and almost every session are spiritual devices in operation against people. These things exist in the spirit realm and have a full impact and real effect on their lives in the natural.

One of the most memorable experiences I had was seeing a device in operation against the soul of a woman that totally crippled her emotional state. She was at the brink of thinking she was completely crazy, analyzing everything and going through a roller coaster of every kind of emotion before finally condemning herself and blaming herself for anything going on in her life or the lives of those around her.

Clearly this was more than being prone to depression or some surface-level state of mind shaped by her surroundings and experiences. There was a much deeper level to this and in this case it proved to be a spiritual problem at the root.

In the spirit realm I saw what looked like an old AM/FM radio that you could tune through a range of frequencies. The only difference was that it had a transmitter on it and was sending signals out. I then saw the lady we were working on, Alison, with a receiver on her head receiving every signal and transmission from this device. (See Fig. 2b)

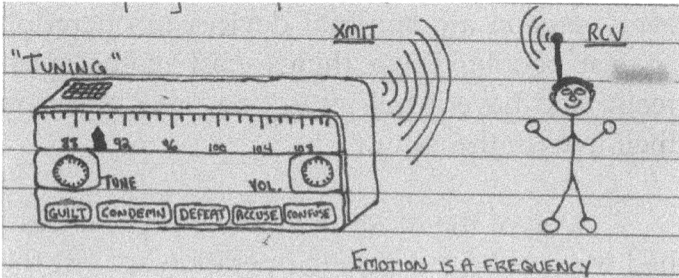

Fig. 2b

This radio transmitter could be tuned to preselected emotions. Some that I saw were guilt, condemnation, defeat, accusation, confusion, etc. There were more, but those were the most popular 'presets' that I saw as buttons on the device.

What a terrible device to be in operation against someone's soul. At any moment, a demon could 'change the station' and send waves of oppressive onslaughts of emotion into her soul based on whatever type of negative emotion it chose.

It was no wonder then that Alison was completely overwhelmed on such a deep emotional level. By all appearances she was crazy – but not because of a particular illness. This was the deepest root of the problem; a demon using a spiritual device against the soul.

Let's pause for a second and try to understand the principle here. All around us, in a much larger scheme of things, is the spirit realm in which these angelic forces reside and carry out their functions, purposes and assignments.

The bible will prove that parts of our soul can be held captive in regions of captivity in hell

– and be severely bound and afflicted by demons.

[Acts 2:27] Because thou wilt not leave my soul in hell, neither wilt thou suffer thine Holy One to see corruption. (KJV)

[Psalm 142:7] Bring my soul out of prison, that I may praise thy name: the righteous shall compass me about; for thou shalt deal bountifully with me. (KJV)

Jesus went to hell upon his death on the cross – and defeated death, hell and the grave. Then He rose again in the resurrection and ascended.

Through Jesus we can attain healing for our souls including parts of our souls being broken out of prison and pulled out of captivity in hell.

'Because you will not leave my soul in hell' is an interesting reference. If one was sent to hell, then they cannot escape. That is a final judgment. Let's make an exception to the rule in the context of God allowing someone to die and experience hell, then pull them up out of it under the condition that they come back to life and preach the testimony of it. Let's call this a near-death experience where a person died for several minutes and was revived. The only other exception is Jesus Christ Himself as part of the master plan for the redemption of mankind.

The Scripture infers that God has the ability to remove a soul from hell under the context of it being in captivity – as though the person were still living and had not yet been judged. 'Bring my soul out of prison' enforces the idea of captivity.

[Psalm 107:10-14] **10** Those who sat in darkness and in the shadow of death, Bound in affliction and irons— **11** Because they rebelled against the words of God, And despised the counsel of the Most High, **12** Therefore He brought down their heart with labor; They fell down, and there was none to help. **13** Then they cried out to the Lord in their trouble, And He saved them out of their distresses. **14** He brought them out of darkness and the shadow of death, And broke their chains in pieces. (NKJV)

Those who are sitting in darkness and dwell in the shadow of death are bound in affliction. Where are these places? Who is binding them? Who is afflicting them? Demons in the spirit realm. Parts of people's souls held captive because of sin, pain and trauma.

[Psalm 18:5] The cords of Sheol (the nether world, the place of the dead) surrounded me; The snares of death confronted me. (AMP)

Perhaps in his distress and woe, a fragment of his soul was captive in hell – whereby being surrounded by the cords of hell, with every snare of death confronting him? Perhaps these sayings were illustrating what was taking place in the spirit realm over his body? And if you read the Scriptures after this passage, you can see how he cried out to God for help and God heard him.

[Isaiah 61:1] … To proclaim release [from confinement and condemnation] to the [physical and spiritual] captives … (AMP)

This Scripture is saying that there can be people bound in confinement within spiritual realms.

[Psalm 142:7] Bring my soul out of prison, that I may praise thy name … (KJV)

Let's look at a Scripture that spells out for us how it is that God shows us these things and also how the Holy Spirit and Jesus plays a part in this.

[John 16:12-13] **12** "I have many more things to say to you, but you cannot bear [to hear] them now. **13** But when He, the Spirit of Truth, comes, He will guide you into all the truth [full and complete truth]. For He will not speak on His own initiative, but He will speak whatever He hears [from the Father—the message regarding the Son] … (AMP)

Jesus had many more things to tell them at that time, but He remained silent about them because the weight and magnitude of the truths those revelations contained were too strong for them to bear. This same principle applies to many people today, who are not ready to receive the fullness of the truth.

Jesus also told us that the Holy Spirit would come and guide us into all truth. In other words, the Holy Spirit would reveal to us these deeper and weighty truths as we became able to bear and understand them.

On top of that, the Holy Spirit isn't speaking on His own initiative but rather only what the Father is telling Him to say.

That sounds like to me the Holy Spirit has a voice and can talk to you regarding these things. It sounds to me like there's a lot more that God wants to speak to us and share with us

– but is unable to do so because of the religious bondage in our minds. I have often been asked what is the best weapon against religious spirits and mindsets? My answer is: Holy Spirit.

A true flow of the Holy Spirit will break down false doctrines and religious spirits and mindsets. Holy Spirit is the best box cutter around; He breaks God out of the boxes people try to stuff Him in.

If you don't like what I'm saying – take it up with God. Let God speak to you Himself about the matter.

[John 16:26-27] **26** In that day you will ask in My name, and I am not saying to you that I will ask the Father on your behalf [because it will be unnecessary]; **27** for the Father Himself [tenderly] loves you, because you have loved Me and have believed that I came from the Father. (AMP)

Why is it unnecessary for Jesus to ask on our behalf any longer? Because God Himself loves us tenderly and we love Jesus and believe that He came from God.

We're no longer an outsider looking in – requiring Jesus to relay every single thing we say, think and do unto the Father as though we were totally and completely cut off from God every moment of our lives.

Through Christ we have the Father, yes, and we are to now develop that personal relationship with Him. Do you mediate with someone, a third party, to talk to your friend or your boss? How about your spouse? Surely not. With God it's the same way – and any part of the Godhead can speak to you. The reason many people refuse to receive this is because it's too much for them to be exposed to a Holy God that convicts them of their sin forcing confrontation against their evil and sinful desires requiring change of heart.

[Luke 8:10] And He said, "To you [who have been chosen] it has been granted to know and recognize the mysteries of the kingdom of God, but to the rest it is in parables, so that though SEEING THEY MAY NOT SEE, AND HEARING THEY MAY NOT UNDERSTAND. (AMP)

Not everyone is called to the deeper things, and they are just fine. God may call them to do different things and ordain them to walk in certain places or levels that aren't too deep – and that is all that is expected out of them. They are not wrong for not having a desire to go deeper; they are exactly where God wants them to be.

[Matthew 13:8] Other seed fell on good soil and yielded grain, some a hundred times as much [as was sown], some sixty [times as much], and some thirty. (AMP)

Some people will only walk on the surface, others will get deep, and some will walk in the very fullness of all that God is and has.

Chapter 4: Breaking Mindsets

I want to go into something that we have experienced in exorcism sessions that has given us quite a depth of understanding in this area.

We have seen demonic spirits affect and possess the souls of people in deep and profound ways, and we have also seen spiritual devices and weapons in effect against people's minds, wills and emotions.

In our experience we have seen generational interjects, soul fragments of other people and alternate personalities coupled with pain and trauma provide deep trenches for demons and curses to lodge themselves within the people.

One thing we have not yet discussed is what we know as a mindset. A mindset is an established set of assumptions, methods or attitudes and beliefs held by a person.

This all came to me after a deliverance session on a person – I was thankful that God set that man free, but I knew he needed more sessions because there was an awful trait to his personality that he over-analyzed and questioned every little detail to the degree God couldn't even flow in Spirit through his vessel.

I said aloud to my wife, "I wish God would show me how to break that thing inside of him, whatever it is." And just then God spoke to me and said these words: "A mindset is more difficult to break than a will."

That statement took me by surprise and I really had to stop and think about what that meant.

As I meditated on that, I could begin to see where a person's will can choose to desire something but eventually be quenched by the more dominant mindset.

For example, a drug addict will desire with their will to come off the drugs when the withdrawals are bad enough – they truly are more than willing to come off their addiction – but then the mindset overrides their will. The mindset, the set of attitudes and beliefs that have been dominant in their thought life and decision making process – the habits of the person – overrides the will because the mindset is a pattern or guideline involving many routines rather than a simple choice of a will.

Here's a biblical example: the Israelite children. God delivered them overnight from hundreds of years of bondage – brought them out of Egypt and crushed all their enemies before them repeatedly with every kind of supernatural miracle power that existed. No one had any reason or right to doubt the power of God or His ability to protect and deliver.

Yet for 40 years God couldn't break the mindsets of bondage off the Israelites and they ended up dying as a result.

Read how many times their wills changed when God's judgment started rolling out in the camp. Every time Moses was summoned to the tent of meeting, it seemed some kind of horrible fate was about to unfold upon the people. Once plagues rolled out and destruction came upon the sin and disobedience then everyone's wills changed and they repented.

But alas, the mindsets remained and eventually brought them back into the same sin patterns. This pattern repeated itself insanely throughout the following books – but we shouldn't judge those Israelites because we do the same thing today.

What I have seen God do in many situations where we are faced with breaking a mindset is that role-playing is a very effective way of ministering a thought process into a person's mind. We are effectively retraining that person to think along a different line or perspective, under the anointing, and are being led by God to establish and introduce new perspectives and realizations into that person's life.

We were working on a girl named Faith that had a mindset that everything was her fault – and that she was accountable and responsible for other people's problems, including her parents.

In her mind, it was her fault that her family had fights and problems. If mom and dad got in an argument and grew distant from each other, then it was her responsibility to fix it and she was accountable if anything happened between them.

After having dealt with demonic spirits inside of her and ministering healing to broken fragments of her soul – there was still something not quite complete about all of it. We came to the conclusion that God did all He could do spiritually for her, and that now what remained was a trained mindset that had to be broken of its repetitive habits.

I started to take several pages of paper and began to tear them out of a notebook. I had about 7 pages torn out before I started to crumple them up one by one. As I crumpled them, I threw them onto the floor of the sanctuary where we work to perform these exorcisms.

Faith was feeling a little uneasy about my making a mess in the house of God – and her mother, who was present but only as an onlooker, was giving me funny looks from behind the row of chairs.

I kept crumpling up papers and throwing them onto the floor around where we were working. I even tore some in half and threw my pen cap near her chair.

I said to Faith, "I'm making a mess in God's house."

At this rate, I really started to wonder what God was doing with me – as I would never entertain the idea of trashing God's house on a normal day. But then again there hasn't been such a thing as a normal day doing these exorcism sessions all the time.

I then asked Faith, "Who's fault is it that I'm making this mess in the Sanctuary? Mine or yours?"

She answered shyly, "Yours". I continued to make a mess. I asked again, "Who do you think ought to clean up this mess? Me or you?"

Because she didn't answer, I knew she was struggling with an internal conflict. Her mindset told her that she ought to clean it up from past experiences and habits. But she knew something was happening here and thought twice before answering. This was good, because it showed that her mind was formulating new routines and pathways in her mindsets to think and behave differently than usual.

I then stood up and started to minister to her, as I began to clean up my mess slowly. I explained that if Faith simply prays to God and places these people in God's hands, and allows Him to work on them and get them to where they need to be – she can relax and trust God and have faith in Him that He is able to fix problems and work things out.

I explained that it was more important for Faith to have a childhood she could enjoy and be concerned about her own self and problems –

leaving adults to deal with their own problems and to be accountable for their own actions.

I told her that she was only responsible for her own actions and problems, and was only accountable for what she knew and what she did with what she knew.

And that if she would just trust God and have faith in Him to deal with the people making a mess around her, trusting God to work on their hearts and cause them to do the right thing that she would soon realize those messes and problems would be gone – and not by her, but by the people who were truly responsible for it.

At this time, I had already cleaned up the mess I made by the time I finished saying all those things. A very enlightened smile grew across her face as she put the two together and realized that I cleaned up the mess I had made and how it went along with what was being ministered to her in the process.

She learned that she only need trust God and have faith, and that God was able to do His job and she didn't have to lift a finger to see that mess go away.

No more false burdens, no more holding herself accountable and responsible for other people's issues. All because of a visual teaching and role playing scenario. But this only worked because it was under the anointing of God and it was the right situation at the right time for everything to click together and break down that mindset and establish a new one.

I have encountered many alternate personalities that surface within the person without them realizing it. Discernment can help you to identify when a person is speaking from their core self or if you are dealing with an alternate personality.

There have been many times that someone was speaking with me and God showed me that I was dealing with an alternate personality... a part of the person that was split or fragmented into pieces that held on to pain and had active defense mechanisms. In such a case, you are still talking to the real person but a different *piece* of them that is holding on to something under the surface. In those times, God gives us the words to speak to those people. Perhaps there is an underlying fear or trauma they are operating from – and there is a slight ministering that has to take place to comfort or reassure that person that all is well with their soul.

Sometimes God can heal those fragments of their soul as you minister to them in love, and the anointing and glory of God restores the person within.

Chapter 5: The Deeper Truths Of The Word

[John 21:25] And there are also many other things which Jesus did, which if they were recorded one by one, I suppose that even the world itself could not contain the books that would be written. (AMP)

We won't be able to trace every situation and every detail back to a Scripture in the bible. The good news however is that the bible contains enough for us to reference and discern the character and nature of God, His works, His ways and His precepts. If we live according to God's desires and walk in the Spirit striving to live Holy – we should be able to hear God when we ask Him ourselves if something is of Him or not.

Not everyone will have a seer anointing or be a prophet to experience all the things in this book for themselves – but for those who have had spiritual experiences or have seen and heard things beyond their understanding, perhaps these revelations could provide insight to what God is doing with you or has shown you previously.

We had a case where we worked on a man named Peter. Peter suffered from guilt, shame and condemnation. Peter had a strong background in denominations that emphasized rituals, regulations and rules and was taught that the gifts of the Spirit were in days of old and no longer existed today.

Working with Peter proved difficult at first, because initially he was convinced that Christians could not have demons. Because he did not believe that fact, those demons didn't have to go anywhere. They all had a legal right to stay inside of him for the simple fact he didn't believe they were there.

We had to minister to Peter under the anointing and God opened his eyes to see the truth about his three part being and how they function and operate with the Spirit of God.

He needed a renewal of his soul to flush out all the condemnation of his past, but that could not happen because he never forgave himself for the things he did wrong.

Not forgiving yourself is just as bad as not forgiving someone else. You are just as much God's creation as anyone else is. And believe it or not, the command to forgive one another does apply to yourself as well.

Not forgiving yourself is just like telling Jesus that what He did on the cross was not enough. You're saying His blood was not worth forgiving yourself – that you would choose to hate what God made you to be, to hate the plan God had for your life and to hate the purpose God made you for. You might as well hate God while you're at it, because His presence is found in your spirit-man and soul. Any time you defile your body with self-hate you are trampling on God's temple.

Oh we thought we only had to forgive others and love others but that somehow it didn't apply to our own selves, even though the word commands us to love one another as we love ourselves.

Or are you saying that it's okay to hate others because you hate yourself and that is following the twisted interpretation of God's word?

We must understand that there are some people who are so bound up, so fragmented and lost on the inside that they are *unable* to help themselves and they require someone to pull them up out of the flames of hell.

[Jude 23] save others, snatching them out of the fire; and on some have mercy but with fear, loathing even the clothing spotted and polluted by their shameless immoral freedom. (AMP)

If those who are in the fire were capable of saving themselves then we wouldn't be commissioned to pluck them out of the dangers of hell. But since we are, it goes without saying that we must utilize what we know to help those around about us as God leads.

The devil doesn't need to possess your entire soul, he only needs one fragment of it to oppress and torment you.

If your soul is your mind, will and emotions then why is it so hard to believe that the enemy can possess and have ownership over a part of your soul held in captivity?

To the naysayers: Is every part of your thought life pure and holy? Every thought and desire? Perhaps you are 95% holy. But boy that 5% that deals with lust is a doozy, isn't it? Everything in your life is perfect except that one area that you seem to struggle with no matter what you try. You just keep on sinning in that area and expecting God's grace to cover you indefinitely. That sounds to me like a portion of your soul (a portion of your mind, will and emotions) that is in bondage to the enemy. You, my friend, may have a fragment of your soul in a prison belonging to Satan.

And the demons are laughing at you because you refuse to believe it! It's win-win for the demons. I have come across quite a few people with this mindset – and though skeptical, they experienced the freedom and release God provided for them for simply yielding to what Jesus was doing for them in this way – liberating and freeing their soul parts from prison. To this day they feel totally different and lighter, more clear, less confusion and chaos. No more strange thoughts, no more sudden impulses or desires that lead to sin. They are free, because of Jesus Christ.

Another person we dealt with was severely afflicted with many soul fragments. In the case of Tammy, soul fragments were injected into her through the laying on of hands by an ascended master who practices witchcraft.

Tammy was at a church service one night and decided to go up for the altar call to deal with pain and wounds inflicted upon her by the pastor, as well as the Body of Christ.

The pastor made a comment to her about how he knew she had a messed up childhood based upon characteristics and traits she exhibited. This wounded Tammy as the rejection and abandonment she suffered from both mother and father was never dealt with.

In an attempt to make this bitterness go away and to release this hurt, she went to the altar and met there a man who was praying for others. She assumed he was part of the church because he was up front praying with people.

She came up to him and asked for prayer and he laid his hand on her head and made the comment that he saw how much "energy" was coming off of her and that he was drawn to her.

As he prayed and laid hands on her body, she said a terrible pain manifested in her stomach to the point she actually let out a scream. After this happened, the man made the comment "Usually when I lay hands on people they cannot contain the fear that manifests within."

At this moment what had taken place was this "soul harvester" had implanted impartations of his own soul inside Tammy to control her. He also deposited fragments of others inside of her – reinforcements that agree with his will.

She said the man who laid hands on her was with another man who stood in the background – and he seemed to be more powerful but just lingered in the background. She said it was as though the man in the background was controlling the man laying hands on people.

The fragments went to work immediately – and influenced Tammy to agree to these two men coming over her house for a lunch appointment with her and her boyfriend. As the men were in her home, they took pictures throughout the house and in all her rooms.

I can assure you this was completely out of character for Tammy to allow these men to enter her home to take pictures for witchcraft purposes. Clearly she was being manipulated and influenced from a foreign or external source.

They prayed throughout the house and then left afterward. Ever since then there has been a lingering darkness in the home and Tammy suffered severe anxiety and panic attacks and lived in total complete fear.

These manifestations occurred so frequently and powerfully that she often felt as though she was having a heart attack and even went to the doctor to have her heart checked.

The doctors saw the increased and accelerated heart rate and said there was no apparent cause for it and they could not figure out why this was happening to her.

Tammy was in a place where she isolated herself from her family because she didn't want them to see her in that condition – a tactic of the enemy to get them alone and isolated without help. She couldn't work because of the anxiety and panic attacks multiple times daily, the jitters and shaking in her body. It made work impossible as her job entailed the use of her steady hands. Another strategy of the enemy – strip the person of their livelihood and support, forcing them to become dependent.

This man was a soul harvester – his goal is to attain fragments of peoples souls and manipulate and control them through witchcraft. He can also inject any of these controlled fragments into others – or even parts of himself.

These people utilize demons to do massive damage to human souls – and these methods and their functionality is very complex and sophisticated.

This man tapped into an unresolved hurt Tammy had at the altar – he deposited fragments into her through the demonic gatekeeper that had access to her soul through the hurt and pain she held onto.

The demons can gain access to a person's soul not only by sin but also through pains and traumas that occur in our lives. For example, a spirit of fear can enter someone after witnessing a brutal crime or a tragic accident. We may not have sinned at that moment – but the trauma opened a door for a spirit to enter and attach to that newly formed wound.

In addition to this, the unresolved abandonment and rejection of her mother and father was a breeding ground for demons that could also be used.

With these fragments in her, they could begin to influence her thoughts and emotions and even her decision making process and will.

His goal was to bombard her with fear and anxiety and attack her faith until it was so worn down and beaten that it could be more easily overcome.

The idea was that she would cave in and seek him for help and guidance in the midst of her woes – with the hope of getting her further into bondage to him with the possibility of exploiting her while destroying God's plan and purpose for her life.

Removing the spirits of fear and anxiety was only a part of the deliverance – even with the spirits gone the soul fragments still had sway and control over her soul and could heavily influence her.

God removed many fragments of souls from her and specifically the ones immersed in witchcraft that knew what they were doing – only when the soul fragments were removed could she experience greater levels of freedom after each session.

The angels of God can be used to bind and arrest or detain the soul fragments. Remember, the Blood of Jesus doesn't necessarily work on a soul fragment because it is a piece of a human mind – not a spirit. But the angels of God have the ability to deal with such fragments.

Soul fragments of others can be spoken to in the same way as alternate personalities (or alters) and can be given a choice to either go back where they came from (in the case that the person is still alive) or it can be released to receive Jesus and go to Heaven or to be escorted into hell.

Because the fragment has a mind, will and set of emotions of its own – it is capable of making a decision by itself. If such a fragment chooses hell or you have to send it there for any other reason – it doesn't mean that person is going to hell. For whatever reason it may already have claim laid upon it by hell (through a legal right, contract, covenant, etc.) and only means that this piece of the person goes back into a region of captivity.

The real person that fragment belongs to needs deliverance and inner healing.

Since God has done these works in her, Tammy reported that the heart racing has dwindled and the crippling fear no longer overpowers her, although she is still going through a deliverance process to finalize the healing process.

It is so important to walk in the Spirit and to discern between what is of God and what is not – and all this trauma was suffered by Tammy simply by someone laying hands on her.

We must be so careful in who we allow to lay hands on us as these things can pass through vessels by the laying on of hands.

We later worked with her boyfriend Kyle, who at one point in his life was so bound up in religious doctrine it was almost impossible to talk to him without getting into a debate.

Kyle looked on at first while his girlfriend Tammy went through all these terrible afflictions. At first he thought she was overreacting and perhaps a little crazy. But as time went on he saw that what was happening to her was supernatural and totally out of character for her.

It wasn't until these soul invaders and demon spirits began to attach themselves to him and caused him to experience the symptoms and afflictions of his girlfriend that he began to understand what was happening here.

Not long after, Kyle showed up for our sessions as well. Through this brief experience, it tore down walls of religion and doctrine and all kinds of mindsets that ultimately would have prevented him from reaching his freedom.

When the Spirit of God hit and the anointing manifested itself, the demons in him began to gyrate his body and cause him to convulse. I commanded the spirits to leave him and depart from his soul and go to the pit in Jesus' name. They came out from him and he was left there after about 15 minutes of manifestations – wondering what on earth just happened to him.

He felt like he was in a war, a rough battle and he was physically drained and exhausted. He could barely lift the water bottle up to his mouth to take a drink! When the session was finished, he was in shock and kept saying how much better he felt but he couldn't wrap his mind around what had just happened. He was stammering as he was walking out of the building with a huge smile on his face, wanting to stay and talk to try and understand but yet wanting to go home and rest at the same time.

He was touched by God that day, as God reached through all those mindsets and broke the yoke of religion and unbelief and caused those spirits to manifest and come out of him.

To this day he has freedom and shares his testimony to others that Christians can have demons and that God does a miraculous work that produces good fruit and freedom in people's lives through deliverance and exorcism.

We also saw a sneaky trick of the enemy at play here – a sort of leapfrog jumper spirit going back and forth. I found it odd that we would see Tammy get set free and then go home to find Kyle bound up with this spirit. Then Kyle would come in and we would see him set free and then the next time Tammy would show up bound with this spirit again.

The Holy Spirit showed us that this spirit (operating with a soul fragment through witchcraft) was jumping from one to the other. We discovered the legal right was at the point of contact of the original event. In other words, the moment the man laid his hands upon Tammy and transferred the fragment through the demonic gatekeeper into her soul because of unresolved bitterness and trauma. Come to find out, the man told her to hold hands with her boyfriend while this was happening. Sure enough it went into the both of them – and the common ground between Tammy and Kyle was bitterness. Different people, different situations, but the same spirit (of bitterness).

Commonality and like-spirits are like welcome signs to demons. A spirit in a person will always seek out common ground and like-spirits in other people to join and connect with. This is why demons couldn't mess Jesus up because Jesus said that the enemy had nothing in Him – in other words, no like-spirits or any common ground to work with.

[John 14:30] … for the ruler of the world (Satan) is coming. And he has no claim on Me [no power over Me nor anything that he can use against Me]; (AMP)

In other words there is nothing that Satan has in his entire kingdom of darkness that could be found in Jesus. No open door, no common ground, no unclean spirit that ever had a way to enter His soul. There was never any guilt in Jesus to give Satan any power over Him, and no corruption in Jesus that would take part with his temptations.

But in the case of Tammy and Kyle, it became evident that this warlock was not easily letting go of either one of them.

One day we were working on Kyle and it just so happened that he brought Tammy with him – which was unusual. She sat in the back of the building by the office while we worked on Kyle in the sanctuary.

During the session I kept seeing visions in my mind of Tammy sitting next to Kyle. I wondered why this kept happening, and after I had opened up in prayer I felt the unction to just be obedient to what apparently God was trying to show me.

I got up and got Tammy, told her to come with me and I sat her down next to Kyle. I anointed the both of them with oil and told them to hold hands together – then I went behind them with bibles in my hand and placed the Word of God on their backs and with the authority of Jesus I commanded every spirit that God had ordained for judgment to get manifested in Jesus' name.

I commanded every soul fragment and invader in the depths of their souls to manifest and go back from whence they came – I released the fire of God and the angels of the Lord to bind, arrest and detain these fragments and spirits and petitioned God to judge them – especially the one that loves to jump back and forth between the two separately.

This time God was having me deliver them both at the same time together, hand-in-hand just like the original moment they were bound up in the same fashion. I began to realize God was re-creating the circumstance of how they were initially bound and setting them free in the same manner.

The spirits manifested strongly in the both of them – it couldn't jump back and forth anymore because they were both right there under the anointing. It was very powerful, and I could feel the hatred of the spirits and the loathing of the soul invader as its strategy was being burned up in the fire of God.

Another victory for Jesus – and this man and woman of God were set free. It was a new experience for me, and I am thankful that God allowed me to participate in this revelation and that He has given me the grace to share it with the Body of Christ and the world.

We experienced quite a display of warfare in a session we did with Dora. In her deliverance session God showed us spiritual weapons of rejection lodged inside of her heart that had to be pulled out and healing ministered to these events and wounds that took place in her life. There was also a record book that an alter was carrying around keeping records of every injustice.

In the natural, the alter would check every word, motive and action that other people displayed toward her against the record book of wrongs and would trigger emotions and feelings from her past that would interfere with and affect the people in her present.

In the process innocent people would be hurt by this alter and it's schemes and defense mechanisms for the sole purpose of 'protecting' the core Dora.

God destroyed these weapons and the alters were released from her mind. After that we saw a vision of a black demon that appeared to be a leader of some type with others under its authority. They were all in this large palace looking building - like a king would have. This spirit had servants, harems, slaves, a cup bearer, etc. We heard "Demonic Patriarch" which meant this spirit was the head of a generational line. We also heard that this spirit was in control of her mind.

God led us to send angels into that palace and bind the patriarch and all its servants. We saw them engage in battle and tear the palace apart going all the way to the throne this demon was sitting on. Underneath the palace there was a dungeon with many prison cells - each cell had a fragment of her soul in captivity. The jailors would go in and torment the fragments and there was no light down there. We called for light to fill the catacombs and release the fragments from the prison cells and angels came and took them out and ministered to them and brought them to the third heaven for restoration and reintegration into the core Dora.

We thought we were done but God wasn't done at all - He showed us a step further beyond. This demon was operating under a larger spiritual structure called the hive mind.

It was a collective consciousness of many fragmented pieces of minds from every family member in this bloodline going back 29 generations. We were blown away that something like this could have even happened - and that's when God explained to us that 29 generations ago there was a man who suffered a great injustice and brooded over it until revenge settled in his heart and he ended up committing murder.

That's where the legal right began for this demonic patriarch to harvest shattered mind fragments into a collective hive and manipulate all kinds of memories, emotions, urges, impulses, etc. and afflict whomsoever it had a legal right to oppress with thoughts and feelings that weren't even their own.

As a result, Dora was being tormented with anger, revenge, retaliation, anti-submissiveness and reproach. (Those were all spirits that were cast out also).

This demonic patriarch had the ability to manipulate and use every one of those fragmented soul parts to come forward and influence Dora's mind, will and emotions. Imagine hundreds of people, ancestors and relatives, all of their thoughts, feelings and desires plaguing your mind causing and influencing you to have various urges, thoughts, desires and inclinations that are not even your own.

Dora probably felt like she was going crazy on this inside with the influx and waves of emotions that would surface within her for no reason at all.

Once the demonic patriarch was bound and on its way out, God proved faithful once again - He showed us what to do to remove the hive mind as well. He showed us a sword that was glowing white and it was called the sword of Truth. We lodged this sword into the queen of the hive's mind fragment and sealed it within.

Then we saw a vision of God's healing and ministering power slowly affect the queen whereby the entire hive followed suit. In the spirit realm this looked like a large brain composed of many fragments of souls. They were all glued together with a sticky substance – but the power of the truth of God's word was causing that adhesive to weaken and melt away, and all the fragments started falling away and glowing, being taken away by angels and restored to wherever they belonged.

The power of God was so amazing to see this huge spiritual architecture being dismantled and restored. These demons set up these kingdoms and systems as though they owned the place and have people in total bondage literally worshiping them and bowing to their every whim - this demon literally sat in a throne with servants and cup bearers with purple royal robes and kingly surroundings. It remained unchallenged for almost 600 years (29 generations) and then because of God, in one moment, angels stormed in and destroyed this place in a matter of minutes.

Many types of bondage that we see in the spirit realm that afflict people are established by demons that have taken up residence inside of their bloodlines for many generations – and the reason they are still there is because they have been totally unchallenged.

Where is the church? What happened to the Body? What would Peter and Paul think about the condition of the church nowadays?

What kind of watered down canned sermon are you hearing? I have seen in the spirit realm a detailed vision God gave to me of the complexity and organization of the kingdom of darkness. I have seen principalities and powers, thrones and dominions, ruler spirits and strongmen over nations, states, counties, cities, towns, neighborhoods, individual households, families and people. It's a giant chess game, for lack of a better description.

You have no idea how organized and powerful the realm of darkness is – sad to say – more organized than the church. And I'm not glorifying the devil here, I'm trying to make you aware of the severity and seriousness of the hour.

I suggest you all put on your big-boy and big-girl pants right now and get ready to swallow this pill:

The wrath of God is imminent upon this nation, America. There is no turning back at this point, and the only good that can be done by intercessors is to slightly mitigate some of the damage – but many things are already written in stone and will simply come to pass just as it is written in Heaven.

Many people's heads will spin and there will be so many questions. I'll tell you the reality is that even though God's hand is behind all of it – the church never had the answer. I'll tell you why – the church was too busy watching television and listening to its iPod, drinking wine with the sin of the world. Too drunk to understand the warning signs blurred out of its peripheral vision as it swerves in between the lanes of religious doctrine and compromise.

A lot of church-goers that you thought were all holy and righteous are actually going to be surprised that there *is* a living God, when He shows up with His judgment. In an instant you'll see the masks crack off their faces and all of the truth about them comes out into the light.

It's at a time like this that the things you've been getting fed all your life start to churn in your stomach – better hope you learned from the Holy Spirit by a true man or woman of God. Whatever you've been digesting all this time is about to come up – and what is it going to produce for you to survive these dark days ahead? Manna from heaven, or a pile of vomit? And don't deceive yourselves, either.

If God were to walk into your bedroom at night, what would He find? What if God went through your computer and DVD collection? What if your partner at work was God, standing by you every minute of the day? How about at home when you think you're behind closed doors? Are you the same exact way in front of all the faces piled into the house of God? How about if God was on a three-way conversation in all your phone calls?

Here's a newsflash – He is, and He does. The fact that you're *still alive* proves that God is merciful and full of grace. The fact that you *still keep on sinning* is nothing short of your own hardened heart and total lack of the fear of God. Don't confuse the two.

When is the last time your pastor taught about how sin of any kind takes you to hell? When was the sermon given about how 'once saved, always saved' is a lie? That God's grace allows us to keep sinning and never change and expect to make heaven our home? How about the lesson your pastor gave about homosexuality? Or did the veil of compromise slowly fall down and cover the face of the church and water down God's Word?

It's awfully convenient isn't it? Lucifer, son of the morning, next highest creature in power from the Godhead, is so easily defeated forever by mere lip service of a self-proclaimed believer because they repeated after someone else in a prayer they don't believe – because if they did they would be living it daily. How wonderful that you'll never suffer and the devil can't touch you forever because you followed the fad of the church on a whim.

The reason your life is cruising on easy street is because you're no threat to the enemy of your soul. He has you right where he wants you, and he won't bother you in your lifetime because he'll have eternity to bother you when you make it to hell.

If your church's bibles have dust on the pages that talk about repentance and sin – you better run for the hills and ask for a dose of the Holy Spirit to knock all of the deception out of your soul.

If you're offended now, then that's good. That means the devil inside of you can't stand the truth and the light that comes from the Word.

[John 3:20] For every wrongdoer hates the Light, and does not come to the Light [but shrinks from it] for fear that his [sinful, worthless] activities will be exposed and condemned. (AMP)

Surely the apostle John couldn't have been talking about you. It must have been for all those other people you happen to judge and gossip about and can't love at all, despite every one of those attributes being sin that takes you to the grave.

What lie have you believed and allowed to become so deeply rooted inside of you that you gloss over every scripture that contradicts your own beliefs? The problem is not the Word of God, it is the uneducated interpreter who has no merits or expertise – because they came into the Word of God with their own flesh, leaning to their own understanding without asking the Holy Spirit to instruct and reveal to them the truth of the Word.

Or did you think that by works and your own efforts you could attain the Kingdom of God? Is it your own sovereignty that allows you to draw a breath? Who made your body and gave you your lungs, and the understanding of how to use them? By whose Spirit was this all made? The same Spirit that was sent to you at Pentecost – constantly knocking at your door, never going against your will like a perfect gentleman; the Holy Spirit.

You open the door for everything and everyone else that loves to destroy you – so why all the deadbolts and security measures on the door the Holy Spirit is knocking on? Meanwhile the devil himself has his feet propped up on your coffee table in your reclining chair, watching your television and listening to your iPod – and you're the one serving him. In your own house.

What exactly is the scope of your vision? Did you think you were here just to be saved and go to heaven? Or have you advanced to a higher rank to come to the realization that God actually had a purpose and detailed plan for your life that you haven't even known about because you don't believe that prophets exist anymore or that God can speak to you and has His own voice?

The truth can sting when it has something to bite and offend. Fortunately for you, it also sets you free. And I believe that because you are a rational person with a sound mind, you would rather be stung and pricked if it meant having your soul saved and making heaven your home.

By the way, taking in all this revelation knowledge has now made you accountable for what you know! And I would advise caution to those that reject what God is showing all of us here throughout this book, because of that simple fact.

[Luke 12:47-48] **47** And that servant who knew his master's will, and yet did not get ready or act in accord with his will, will be beaten with many lashes [of the whip], **48** but the one who did not know it and did things worthy of a beating, will receive only a few [lashes]. From everyone to whom much has been given, much will be required; and to whom they entrusted much, of him they will ask all the more. (AMP)

The reason I am not holding back any punches with the truth is because the devil doesn't hold back any punches when it comes to anything he does. He's out to attack you full force to destroy you and take you to hell. My question is why isn't the majority of the Body of Christ teaching spiritual warfare, deliverance, exorcism, striving to live holy, walking in the Spirit, utilizing the gifts of the Spirit and recognizing the prophetic?

Yes, each church has its purpose according to God. There is nothing wrong with a nice, quiet 30-fold church singing hymns and preaching grace. That is wonderful for all the people who peak at that level and enjoy the Lord and love God with all their hearts and will one day sit in heavenly places.

I'm talking about the ones who are equipped but refuse to walk out the fullness of what they are destined to do. There is not enough warfare going on across the entire Body of Christ – not a strong enough bond of unity.

If you can't believe anything thus far, then believe this testimony – I was an ex-Satanist who knows and understands the power of witchcraft and demons. I know what a fight is with the enemy – and quite often the demons that manifest in our sessions know me by name and call me out as a traitor and I fight every day the demonic warfare of having once served the devil and now serving Jesus Christ in addition to the calling God has on my life coupled with the separate warfare that comes from deliverance and exorcism – straight walking into the devil's territory and taking back what he stole. Plucking souls out of his grasp by the power of Jesus Christ and His authority.

I know very well what it's like to live what I teach and experience it each day. I'm not giving you my resume and I'm not puffing any part of my life up – I am praying that what you know of me will minister to you or someone you know to bring about healing and deliverance or even salvation to you or those around you. God said He would use my past in its fullness to reach souls and I hope that is taking place.

The only reason I am still alive to teach and give this testimony is because of the pure grace of God alone. None of this is anything that I did, but rather the Holy Spirit through me.

I hope and pray that this book will give insight to you to show and illustrate deeper truths from God's word and how the realm of deliverance and exorcism works behind the scenes. I pray that God's wisdom may fall upon you to help you and those around you from bondages of the enemy – in Jesus' name, amen.

www.ingramcontent.com/pod-product-compliance
Lightning Source LLC
Chambersburg PA
CBHW070537030426
42337CB00016B/2244